THE SPECTATOR

CARTOON BOOK

Edited by
Michael Heath

P

PROFILE BOOKS

in association with

The Spectator

First published
in book form in Great Britain in 2003 by
Profile Books Ltd
58A Hatton Garden, London EC1N 8LX
in association with
The Spectator
56 Doughty Street, London WC1N 2LL

Typeset by MacGuru
info@macguru.org.uk

Printed and bound in Great Britain by
Bookmarque Ltd, Croydon, Surrey

A CIP catalogue record for this book is available from
the British Library.

ISBN 1 86197 602 X

'I just love fast food.'

'You put your third lower left leg in, you put your third lower left leg out, in, out, in, out, you shake it all about …'

'Oh, don't go — I promise, one more drink
and you'll find me attractive.'

'I'm a student!'

'You've been crying again haven't you?'

'I cant' take your coldness anymore, Peter.'

'Well, it's not my idea of a second opinion!!'

*'Oh, for heaven's sake, Nigel,
the boy's only having a few soldiers.'*

'Can't talk now, I'm about to go through a tunnel.'

'He's right you know, there should be an apostrophe.'

'You really are walking out on me this time,
aren't you Caroline?'

'It's got someone's tongue.'

HANNIBAL CROSSING THE ALPS

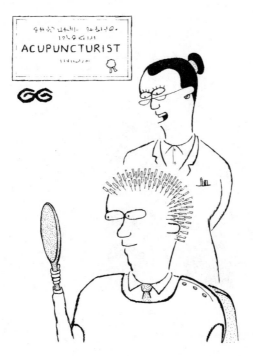

'It doesn't cure baldness, but it sure is a vast improvement.'

'Fill me in — who's detox and who's Botox?'

'Business is really good …
I had to hire someone to laugh all the way to the bank.'

'Blast … no … no … damn …'

'He did retire, but his severance package was so big he bought the company.'

'You should floss every morning!'

'I used to be an urban fox but then I thought I'd get the best of both worlds and commute.'

'Oh, dear, I'm awfully sorry.'

'You always said you wanted to go out in style, Phoebe.'

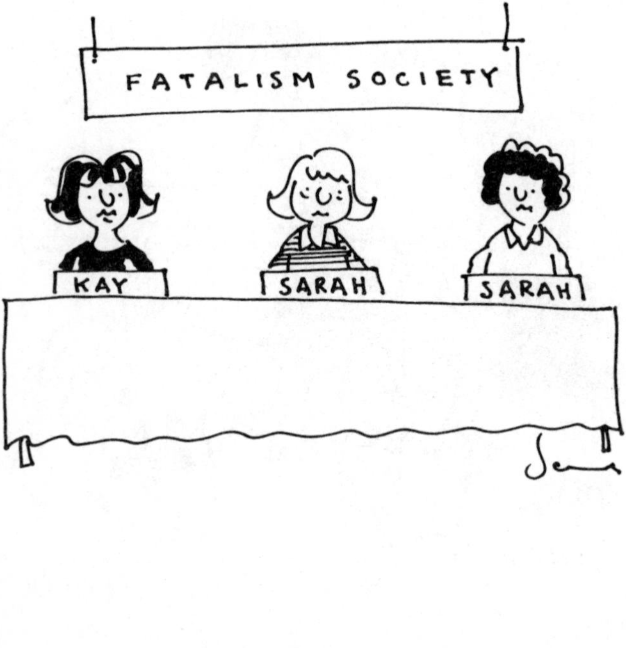
FATALISM SOCIETY
KAY
SARAH
SARAH

'And if the feathers don't impress you I just want you to know that I own a Porsche.'

'I don't like the look of this.'

'Is there any way of keeping the light on when you're inside?'

'Oh no, it's the Grim Peeper!'

'You've been fighting again haven't you, son?'

'I knew I shouldn't get support tights!'

'I'm a silkworm.'

'So we're all agreed we need to tighten our belts, pull up our socks and Miss Riggins needs to shorten her skirts …'

'I prefer to come into the bank personally rather than those awful automated phone lines.'

'I sometimes think we spoil that dog.'

'I paid for all my wife's fitness club, all her jogging gear and a personal trainer — and she's done a runner.'

'George, he'll talk when he's ready.'

'Actually, your glasses may take more than an hour.'

'How do I know they're yours?'

'Customs and Excise, Mr Wills.
It's about your home-made wine …'

'It's from AMNESTY INTERNATIONAL for you.'

'Nice Titians!'

'You spoil those sharks.'

'No you can't be a lawyer. It's handbag or shoes, that's it.'

'She must be home, the phone's still warm.'

'We adopted.'

'Ah look, he wants his dinner.'

'You know how you've always wanted a dream kitchen?'

'I'm sorry — I thought you ordered the Lobster Nuremburg.'

'This one put up a real fight, but I got him in the end.'

'And the wife uses that one for popping to the shops.'

*Embarrassingly, Jack's birthday wish
came true straight away*

THE SHOCK OF THE OLD

*'Ron's managed to stop smoking
but he's put on an awful lot of weight.'*

'Do you ever wish you'd died young?'

'It's the parrot … he says to remember his seed.'

'Hello … oh hi … not so bad, how's yourself?'

'What a performance over a bone.'

'Advantage Miss Barakova.'